STARTUP FROM SCRATCH

Launching a Business in 90 Days

Wayne Roland

Table of Contents

INTRODUCTION

Embarking on the journey of building a startup from scratch is a bold endeavor that requires unwavering determination, strategic planning, and rapid execution. The concept of launching a business in just 90 days might seem audacious, yet it has become a testament to the agility and innovation that characterize the modern entrepreneurial landscape. This condensed timeline forces aspiring entrepreneurs to prioritize the essentials, cut through red tape, and swiftly adapt to changes in the market.

In this era of fast-paced technological advancement and shifting consumer demands, the traditional approach to business launch has evolved. The 90-day startup model emphasizes lean strategies, leveraging available resources judiciously, and focusing on the minimum viable product (MVP) to enter the market quickly. This approach not only reduces financial risks but also enables founders to gather real-world feedback that informs further development.

However, the path to building a business in such a short span is riddled with challenges. Crafting a viable business plan, securing initial funding, developing a compelling brand identity, and establishing an online presence are just a few of the hurdles. Additionally, nurturing a cohesive team and cultivating a resilient company culture within this accelerated timeframe requires adept leadership and efficient decision-making.

This series delves into the intricacies of the 90-day startup journey, exploring the key steps, pivotal decisions, and fundamental strategies that can contribute to a successful launch. Assembling insights from experienced entrepreneurs, industry experts, and real-world case studies, we uncover the art of transforming a novel idea into a tangible, thriving business within a mere three months.

CHAPTER ONE

The 90-Day Startup Paradigm: Launching a Business in a Tight Timeframe

In the dynamic landscape of entrepreneurship, where innovation is ceaseless and competition fierce, the notion of launching a business within a mere 90 days has gained prominence as a testament to adaptability, agility, and resourcefulness. This chapter delves into the intriguing world of the 90-day startup paradigm, illuminating its origins, shedding light on its benefits and challenges, and uncovering the mindset essential for entrepreneurs to not only navigate but thrive in this accelerated journey.

Origins of the 90-Day Startup Approach

Traditionally, the process of launching a business involved meticulous planning, prolonged development cycles, and exhaustive market research. However, as technology accelerated, consumer behavior evolved, and barriers to entry diminished, a new approach emerged—one that embraced speed, flexibility, and immediate market presence. The 90-day startup paradigm can be traced back to the Lean Startup methodology, popularized by Eric Ries, which champions iterative product development, validated learning, and fast feedback loops. This approach, coupled with the "fail fast, fail forward" philosophy, laid the foundation for entrepreneurs to test their assumptions quickly and refine their offerings in real-time.

Benefits of the 90-Day Approach

1. Rapid Market Entry

One of the most compelling benefits of the 90-day startup paradigm is the ability to enter the market swiftly. Traditional business launch processes could take months or even years, during which market dynamics could change dramatically. By compressing the timeline, entrepreneurs can capitalize on emerging opportunities and stay ahead of competitors.

2. Focus on Essentials

In a constrained time frame, entrepreneurs are forced to prioritize essentials. This leads to streamlined decision-making, efficient resource allocation, and a sharper focus on the core value proposition of the business. The 90-day approach compels founders to cut through the noise and concentrate on what truly matters.

3. Reduced Financial Risk

Longer development cycles often result in higher costs and increased financial risk. With the 90-day paradigm, startups can bring a minimum viable product (MVP) to market quickly, gauge user feedback, and make necessary adjustments without overcommitting resources. This approach significantly mitigates financial risks associated with prolonged development.

4. Iterative Learning

Embracing a rapid timeline encourages a culture of continuous learning. Entrepreneurs can test assumptions, gather real-world data, and iterate on their offerings based on tangible feedback. This iterative learning process not only improves the product but also refines the overall business strategy.

5. Early Customer Engagement

The 90-day approach facilitates early customer engagement. Entrepreneurs have the opportunity to involve potential customers in the product development process from the outset. This not only creates a sense of ownership but also increases the likelihood of customer adoption upon launch.

Challenges of the 90-Day Approach

1. Intense Time Pressure
The primary challenge of the 90-day startup paradigm is the intense time pressure it imposes. Entrepreneurs must navigate through ideation, validation, product development, marketing, and launch within a fraction of the time typically allocated. This can lead to burnout and potential compromises in quality.

2. Limited Room for Error
With such a short timeframe, mistakes can have amplified consequences. There is little margin for error, and any misstep could impact the success of the business launch. This demands a meticulous approach to planning and execution.

3. Resource Constraints
Entrepreneurs working within the 90-day framework often face resource constraints. Limited time may translate to limited access to funding, skilled team members, and other critical resources. Creative problem-solving becomes essential to make the most of available assets.

4. Unrealistic Expectations
While the 90-day approach can yield remarkable outcomes, it is not a guarantee of instant success.

Unrealistic expectations about the speed of growth and market penetration can lead to disappointment if the business doesn't achieve desired results within the abbreviated timeline.

The Mindset of a 90-Day Entrepreneur

The success of a startup in the 90-day paradigm hinges on the entrepreneurial mindset. The following attributes are crucial for entrepreneurs embracing this approach:

1. Agility and Adaptability
Entrepreneurs must be willing to pivot swiftly based on market feedback. Flexibility in changing course and adapting to new information is vital to make the most of the condensed timeline.

2. Resilience
The 90-day journey is demanding and filled with challenges. Entrepreneurs need to cultivate resilience to navigate setbacks, learn from failures, and keep moving forward with unwavering determination.

3. Focus on Value
With limited time, entrepreneurs must focus on delivering real value to their customers. This requires understanding the pain points of the target

audience and tailoring the product to meet those needs effectively.

4. Collaboration and Delegation
A successful 90-day startup requires effective teamwork. Entrepreneurs should be adept at delegating tasks, leveraging the strengths of team members, and fostering a collaborative environment.

5. Rapid Decision-Making
In the world of the 90-day startup, there's no room for prolonged decision-making processes. Entrepreneurs must make informed decisions quickly, relying on a combination of data, intuition, and industry expertise.

Embracing the Challenge

The 90-day startup paradigm is not for the faint of heart, but for those willing to embrace the challenge, it holds the potential for rapid growth, innovation, and market disruption. By understanding the origins, benefits, and challenges of this approach, and by cultivating the necessary mindset, entrepreneurs can embark on a journey that defies traditional timelines and paves the way for a new era of agile and resilient startups. This chapter serves as a foundation for the subsequent exploration of ideation, validation, lean planning, execution, branding, and marketing within the context of the 90-day startup journey.

CHAPTER TWO

Ideation and Validation: Building the Cornerstone of Your 90-Day Startup

In the dynamic landscape of startup entrepreneurship, the journey from concept to reality begins with a single spark of innovation. The foundation of any successful startup is a solid idea—one that addresses a pressing problem, fulfills an unmet need, or introduces a groundbreaking solution to a market. This chapter delves into the critical phases of ideation and validation within the context of the 90-day startup paradigm. We explore effective techniques to generate ideas, methods to swiftly validate those ideas, the significance of identifying a target audience, and the pivotal role of market research and early customer feedback.

The Art of Ideation: Nurturing Creativity

Ideation Techniques:
The ideation process is the birthplace of groundbreaking concepts. Entrepreneurs embarking on the 90-day startup journey must employ creative techniques that foster innovation. Brainstorming sessions, mind mapping, and lateral thinking exercises are valuable tools that encourage out-of-the-box thinking. Furthermore, drawing inspiration from diverse sources—such as everyday

problems, personal experiences, emerging trends, and technological advancements—can lead to unique and viable business ideas.

Problem-Centric Approach:
Startups that address real-world problems have a higher likelihood of success. Adopting a problem-centric approach involves identifying pain points and challenges that potential customers face. Entrepreneurs must empathize with their target audience, putting themselves in their shoes to gain insights that drive idea generation.

Swift Validation: From Concept to Reality

The Minimum Viable Product (MVP).
In the accelerated timeline of the 90-day startup, speed is paramount. Entrepreneurs must focus on developing a Minimum Viable Product (MVP)—a simplified version of their idea that showcases its core value proposition. The MVP allows startups to quickly enter the market, test their assumptions, and gather real-world feedback that informs further development.

Lean Validation Methods.
Lean validation methods, inspired by the Lean Startup methodology, prioritize rapid learning and iterative development. Techniques such as creating

landing pages, mockups, and prototypes provide a tangible representation of the idea without a full-scale investment. These tools facilitate early engagement with potential customers and validate interest before significant resources are allocated.

Pilot Programs and Beta Testing.
For startups with ideas that can be piloted or tested in a controlled environment, pilot programs and beta testing offer valuable validation opportunities. These programs allow entrepreneurs to work closely with a smaller group of users, observe their interactions, and refine the offering based on real-time feedback.

The Target Audience: The Guiding North Star

Identifying Your Ideal Customer.
Defining a clear target audience is paramount to the success of any startup. Startups must ask themselves: Who will benefit the most from our solution? What demographics, preferences, and pain points define this audience? This not only guides product development but also shapes marketing strategies and messaging.

Creating Customer Personas.
Customer personas are detailed profiles that encapsulate the characteristics and behaviors of the

target audience. Developing these personas helps entrepreneurs understand their customers' motivations, challenges, and preferences. This insight informs decision-making throughout the startup journey.

Niche vs. Mass Market.
In the 90-day startup paradigm, it's often wiser to focus on a specific niche within the broader market. Niche markets allow startups to tailor their offerings to a concentrated audience, making it easier to address specific needs and establish a foothold before expanding to a larger market.

The Role of Market Research and Early Feedback

Market Research.
Thorough market research is the compass that guides startup endeavors. Entrepreneurs must analyze industry trends, competitors, potential barriers, and opportunities. This research provides a comprehensive understanding of the market landscape and informs strategies for differentiation and growth.

Customer Discovery Interviews.
Engaging in customer discovery interviews is a valuable method to collect insights directly from

potential customers. These interviews provide a deeper understanding of customer pain points, preferences, and willingness to adopt new solutions. The feedback gained from these conversations shapes product development and helps tailor the offering to customer needs.

Pivoting and Iteration.
The data collected through market research and early feedback often lead to pivotal insights. Entrepreneurs must be willing to pivot their ideas or adjust their strategies based on new information. This adaptive approach is fundamental to the lean methodology and allows startups to stay aligned with market demands.

Conclusion
The 90-day startup journey begins with a compelling idea and is fueled by swift validation and meticulous understanding of the target audience. Effective ideation techniques, lean validation methods, and customer-centric approaches are the cornerstones of success. Entrepreneurs must be willing to listen, learn, and adapt as they transform their ideas into tangible solutions that address real-world challenges. By embracing these principles, startups can navigate the complexities of the rapid startup timeline and

lay a strong foundation for growth and innovation. In the subsequent chapters, we explore how lean planning, efficient execution, branding, marketing, and embracing the entrepreneurial mindset contribute to the realization of a thriving business within the condensed 90-day window.

CHAPTER THREE

Lean Planning and Strategy: Navigating the 90-Day Startup Landscape

In the realm of startup entrepreneurship, the traditional approach to business planning often collides with the accelerated timeline of the 90-day startup paradigm. While conventional business plans entail exhaustive market analyses, detailed financial projections, and comprehensive strategies, the constraints of the 90-day journey demand a more agile and streamlined planning approach. This chapter delves into the world of lean planning and strategy—a methodology tailored to the rapid pace of startup launch. We explore how entrepreneurs can define a clear value proposition, set achievable goals, outline a Minimum Viable Product (MVP), and devise a streamlined strategy that fosters efficient execution within the confines of 90 days.

The Essence of Lean Planning

Adaptability Over Rigidity.
Unlike traditional business plans, which often require significant upfront investment of time and resources, lean planning is about adaptability and flexibility. Entrepreneurs in the 90-day startup realm cannot afford to be bound by rigid plans that

might quickly become obsolete. Instead, lean planning emphasizes an iterative process that accommodates shifts in the market and new insights gained through real-world feedback.

Embracing the MVP Concept.
At the core of lean planning is the concept of the Minimum Viable Product (MVP). In the 90-day startup journey, creating an MVP allows entrepreneurs to swiftly bring a scaled-down version of their idea to market. This MVP serves as a vehicle for testing assumptions, gathering feedback, and refining the product based on tangible user interactions.

Focus on Essential Elements.
Lean planning prioritizes the identification and development of essential elements that align with the core value proposition. Unnecessary features or components are set aside in favor of creating a streamlined product that addresses the primary needs of the target audience. This approach ensures efficient resource utilization within the time frame.

Defining a Clear Value Proposition

Understanding the Problem.
Startups that succeed are those that address real problems. In the lean planning context,

entrepreneurs must thoroughly understand the pain points and challenges their target audience faces. This understanding lays the groundwork for crafting a value proposition that resonates deeply with potential customers.

Crafting the Value Proposition.
The value proposition concisely communicates how a startup's product or service solves a specific problem or fulfills a need for its customers. In the 90-day startup journey, this proposition must be honed to its essence, highlighting the unique benefits and differentiation points that set the offering apart from competitors.

Setting Achievable Goals

SMART Goals.
In the realm of lean planning for 90-day startups, goals must be SMART: Specific, Measurable, Achievable, Relevant, and Time-bound. These goals provide a clear roadmap for the startup's direction and help measure progress along the way. Each goal should be broken down into smaller, actionable steps to ensure steady advancement.

Focus on Key Metrics.
With a condensed timeline, startups cannot afford to chase an exhaustive list of metrics. Instead,

entrepreneurs should identify key performance indicators (KPIs) that align with their goals and focus on tracking these indicators closely. This laser-focused approach ensures that efforts are directed toward the most impactful areas.

Outlining the Minimum Viable Product (MVP)

The Power of Simplification.
Creating an MVP requires a deliberate process of simplification. Entrepreneurs must strip away non-essential features and functionalities to distill the product down to its core value. This approach not only expedites development but also reduces the risk of over-engineering.

Validating Assumptions.
The MVP serves as a hypothesis to validate assumptions about the market's needs and preferences. By releasing the MVP to a limited audience, entrepreneurs can gather data on user behavior, preferences, and pain points. This data-driven validation informs the subsequent development and iteration phases.

Devising a Streamlined Strategy

The Role of Strategy.
In the 90-day startup journey, a streamlined strategy is the compass that guides efficient

execution. A well-defined strategy encompasses aspects such as product development, marketing, distribution, and customer engagement. It outlines how the startup will achieve its goals within the compressed timeline.

Agile Methodology.
The lean startup methodology places great emphasis on agility. Entrepreneurs must embrace the principles of continuous iteration, quick adaptation, and learning from failures. An agile strategy allows startups to respond to market feedback swiftly and refine their approach in real-time.

Resource Allocation and Prioritization.
Resource constraints are inherent in the 90-day startup paradigm. Entrepreneurs must allocate resources judiciously, focusing on activities that have the greatest impact on achieving the defined goals. This requires making tough decisions about where to invest time, money, and effort.

Conclusion.
Lean planning and strategy are not just adaptations to the 90-day startup paradigm; they are foundational to its success. Entrepreneurs who embrace the principles of lean planning understand

the importance of adaptability, efficient resource utilization, and relentless focus on value. By defining a clear value proposition, setting achievable goals, outlining an MVP, and devising a streamlined strategy, startups can navigate the challenges of the rapid startup timeline with confidence. In the subsequent chapters, we explore the crucial aspects of execution, team collaboration, branding, and marketing that contribute to the realization of a thriving business within the confines of 90 days.

CHAPTER FOUR

Resource Mobilization and Funding: Navigating Financial Waters in the 90-Day Startup

Launching a startup within the condensed time frame of 90 days requires more than just a groundbreaking idea and a well-defined strategy. Adequate resources, particularly funding, play a pivotal role in turning concepts into tangible realities. This chapter delves into the complex world of resource mobilization and funding within the context of the 90-day startup paradigm. We explore a range of funding options tailored to this accelerated timeline, including bootstrapping, crowdfunding, angel investment, and accelerators. Moreover, we offer insights into crafting a compelling pitch that resonates with potential investors and tips for attracting early financial support.

The Crucial Role of Funding

Fueling Growth and Development.
Funding provides the lifeline for startups, enabling them to cover operational expenses, product development costs, marketing efforts, and talent acquisition. For startups aiming to launch within

90 days, securing funding becomes even more critical due to the limited timeframe for execution.

Capitalizing on Opportunities.
In the rapidly evolving startup landscape, seizing timely opportunities can be a game-changer. Adequate funding empowers startups to capitalize on emerging trends, respond to market demands, and establish a competitive edge swiftly.

Funding Options for the 90-Day Timeline

Bootstrapping: Self-Sufficiency as a Foundation.
Bootstrapping, or self-funding, involves utilizing personal savings, revenue generated from early sales, or minimal external resources to launch the startup. While bootstrapping requires careful financial management, it provides founders with complete control over their vision and allows for agile decision-making.

Crowdfunding: Harnessing the Power of the Crowd. Crowdfunding platforms offer startups the opportunity to raise funds from a large number of individuals, often in exchange for early access to products or other incentives. This approach not only secures funding but also validates market interest and gathers an initial customer base.

Angel Investment: Guided by Experienced Backers.
Angel investors are high-net-worth individuals who provide capital to startups in exchange for equity or convertible debt. Beyond financial support, angel investors often offer mentorship, industry expertise, and valuable connections that can accelerate growth.

Accelerators: Intensive Support for Rapid Growth.
Startup accelerators are programs designed to fast-track early-stage companies. In addition to funding, they provide mentorship, resources, and networking opportunities. Participating in an accelerator can help startups refine their ideas, enhance their MVPs, and establish a solid foundation for growth.

Crafting a Compelling Pitch

A Story of Vision and Impact.
A compelling pitch goes beyond financial projections and data—it tells a story that resonates with potential investors. Entrepreneurs must articulate their vision, explain the problem they're solving, and highlight the impact their solution will have on the market and customers.

Demonstrating Market Understanding.
Investors want to see that entrepreneurs understand the market dynamics and have a clear understanding of their target audience. A pitch should convey the market's pain points, the startup's unique value proposition, and the strategies for capturing market share.

Highlighting Traction and Validation.
For startups operating on a 90-day timeline, showcasing early traction and validation is crucial. This could include pre-orders, partnerships, customer testimonials, or successful pilot programs. Investors are more likely to invest when they see evidence of demand and interest.

Attracting Early Investors

Building Relationships and Networks.
Networking plays a pivotal role in attracting early investors. Entrepreneurs should actively participate in startup events, industry conferences, and networking groups to connect with potential backers. Building relationships early can lead to investment opportunities down the line.

Leveraging Online Platforms.
Online platforms, such as LinkedIn, AngelList, and startup forums, provide avenues for entrepreneurs

to showcase their ideas and connect with investors. Maintaining a strong online presence and sharing insights about the startup journey can pique the interest of potential backers.

Seeking Warm Introductions.
Warm introductions from trusted connections can significantly increase the chances of getting in front of potential investors. Entrepreneurs should leverage their networks to secure introductions and recommendations from individuals who can vouch for their credibility.

Due Diligence and Building Trust

Transparency and Honesty.
Investors perform due diligence to assess the viability of a startup. Entrepreneurs should be transparent about the startup's progress, challenges, and financial situation. Honesty builds trust and demonstrates a commitment to success.

Preparing for Investor Questions.
Investors will have probing questions about the startup's market, competition, business model, and growth strategy. Entrepreneurs should anticipate these questions and have well-researched, thoughtful answers at the ready.

Legal and Financial Preparedness.
Before seeking investment, startups must ensure they have proper legal and financial structures in place. This includes having a clear equity ownership structure, well-drafted investment agreements, and a thorough understanding of the financial aspects of the business.

Conclusion

Securing initial funding within the constraints of a 90-day startup timeline requires entrepreneurs to be resourceful, strategic, and persuasive. By exploring funding options tailored to the accelerated journey, crafting compelling pitches that resonate with investors, and building relationships with potential backers, startups can navigate the financial landscape successfully. This chapter lays the groundwork for the subsequent exploration of execution strategies, team dynamics, branding, marketing, and the entrepreneurial mindset, all of which contribute to the realization of a thriving business within the dynamic 90-day window.

CHAPTER FIVE

Execution and Iteration: Breathing Life into the 90-Day Startup Vision

In the whirlwind of startup entrepreneurship, ideas alone are insufficient. Execution—the process of turning those ideas into tangible products or services—is where the rubber meets the road. Within the confines of the 90-day startup paradigm, efficient execution takes on a heightened significance. This chapter delves into the intricacies of execution and iteration, outlining strategies for assembling a focused team, allocating tasks effectively, and managing the development process. It underscores the importance of agile methodologies, continuous iteration, and the art of adapting to market feedback to refine the Minimum Viable Product (MVP) within the condensed timeframe.

The Imperative of Efficient Execution

From Vision to Reality.
Execution transforms abstract concepts into concrete offerings. Entrepreneurs must align their vision with practical steps to ensure that the startup's product or service takes shape and becomes market-ready within the 90-day window.

Maximizing Speed and Impact.
In the fast-paced world of the 90-day startup, efficiency is paramount. Startups must aim to achieve maximum impact with minimal resources. Efficient execution entails clear communication, strategic decision-making, and a well-coordinated team effort.

Building a Focused and Agile Team

Skill Diversity and Complementary Strengths.
Assembling the right team is a cornerstone of successful execution. Entrepreneurs should seek team members whose skill sets complement one another. Diversity of expertise—ranging from technical proficiency to marketing acumen—is essential for addressing multifaceted challenges.

Shared Vision and Dedication.
A cohesive team is built on a shared vision for the startup's success. Team members must be aligned with the startup's goals and exhibit dedication to the common mission. Mutual trust and open communication form the bedrock of collaboration.

Agile Mindset and Adaptability.
In the 90-day startup journey, an agile mindset is indispensable. Team members should be adaptable and willing to pivot quickly based on emerging

insights and market feedback. Flexibility enables rapid course correction when necessary.

Allocating Tasks Effectively

Prioritization and Resource Allocation.
With time as the most limited resource, prioritization is key. Entrepreneurs must allocate tasks based on their impact on the MVP and the startup's overall goals. Tasks that contribute directly to the core value proposition take precedence.

Divide and Conquer.
Breaking down complex tasks into smaller, manageable components is an effective approach. Entrepreneurs can assign these components to team members based on their expertise, streamlining the execution process and ensuring progress on multiple fronts.

Task Ownership and Accountability.
Each task should have a designated owner responsible for its successful completion. Establishing clear lines of ownership fosters accountability and ensures that tasks are tracked and executed efficiently.

Embracing Agile Methodologies

Agile Principles for Rapid Development.
Agile methodologies, originally popularized in software development, have become a cornerstone of efficient startup execution. Principles such as iterative development, frequent testing, and continuous feedback align seamlessly with the 90-day timeline.

Iterative Development and Prototyping.
Iterative development involves building the MVP incrementally, continually adding features and enhancements based on ongoing feedback. Prototyping allows entrepreneurs to visualize the product early on and make necessary adjustments before investing substantial resources.

Frequent Testing and Adaptation.
In the 90-day startup journey, testing cannot wait until the final stages. Frequent testing of individual components or features enables rapid identification of flaws and areas for improvement. This approach reduces the likelihood of major setbacks and accelerates development.

Adapting to Market Feedback

The Role of Early Customers.

Early customers are invaluable sources of feedback. Their interactions with the MVP provide insights into usability, functionality, and potential pain points. Entrepreneurs should actively seek and listen to this feedback to inform iterative improvements.

Balancing Vision and Feedback

While feedback is essential, entrepreneurs must strike a balance between adhering to their vision and incorporating valuable insights. The challenge lies in recognizing when to pivot based on feedback and when to stay true to the startup's core value proposition.

Refining the MVP

The MVP is not a static entity; it evolves based on feedback and market dynamics. Entrepreneurs should be prepared to make adjustments, add features, or even pivot the offering entirely if market feedback suggests a better direction.

Navigating Challenges and Maintaining Momentum

Overcoming Roadblocks.
In the fast-paced 90-day startup journey, challenges are inevitable. Entrepreneurs must approach challenges as opportunities for growth and innovation. Creative problem-solving and resilience are essential for maintaining momentum.

Staying Motivated and Focused.
The 90-day timeline can be intense, and fatigue can set in. Entrepreneurs must find ways to stay motivated and maintain focus. Setting milestones, celebrating small wins, and fostering a supportive team culture contribute to sustained energy.

Continuous Learning and Improvement.
Execution is a continuous learning process. Entrepreneurs should actively seek insights from both successes and failures, adapting strategies and practices based on real-world outcomes.

Conclusion

In the dynamic landscape of startup entrepreneurship, execution is the driving force that transforms dreams into reality. Within the confines of the 90-day startup paradigm, efficient execution becomes a non-negotiable imperative. By assembling a focused and agile team, allocating tasks effectively, embracing agile methodologies, and adapting to market feedback, entrepreneurs can bring their Minimum Viable Product (MVP) to life in a way that resonates with their target audience. This chapter lays the foundation for the subsequent exploration of branding, marketing, team dynamics, and the entrepreneurial mindset—elements that contribute to the realization of a thriving business within the dynamic 90-day window.

CHAPTER SIX

Branding, Marketing, and Launch: Shaping Your 90-Day Startup's Identity

In the bustling world of startup entrepreneurship, the path from ideation to execution culminates in the pivotal moment of launch. Within the confines of the 90-day startup paradigm, a successful launch is not only a culmination of efforts but also a reflection of strategic branding and effective marketing. This chapter delves into the intricacies of branding, marketing, and launch, emphasizing their role in shaping the startup's identity, establishing a strong online presence, and crafting a compelling narrative that resonates with the target audience. From creating a distinct brand identity to planning a strategic marketing campaign, we explore how these elements contribute to a triumphant launch within the dynamic 90-day window.

The Essence of Branding in Startup Success

The Power of Perception.
Branding goes beyond just a logo or color scheme; it encompasses the perception and emotions that a startup evokes in its audience. In the 90-day startup journey, branding serves as the foundation

for all marketing efforts, creating a cohesive and memorable identity.

Defining the Brand Identity.
Entrepreneurs must distill their startup's values, mission, and unique value proposition into a clear and concise brand identity. This identity sets the stage for how the startup is perceived by customers and differentiates it from competitors.

Consistency Across Touchpoints.
In the fast-paced world of the 90-day startup, maintaining consistency across all touchpoints is crucial. From the website to social media to marketing materials, a consistent brand identity fosters trust and recognition.

Establishing an Online Presence

Creating an Impactful Website.
A startup's website is often the first point of contact for potential customers. In the 90-day timeline, entrepreneurs must focus on creating a clean, user-friendly website that effectively communicates the brand identity and value proposition.

Leveraging Social Media.
Social media platforms provide a cost-effective means of reaching a wide audience. Entrepreneurs

should strategically choose platforms that align with their target demographic and develop content that resonates with their interests and pain points.

Content Strategy for Engagement.
A content strategy ensures that the startup consistently delivers valuable content to its audience. In the 90-day startup journey, content—such as blog posts, videos, and infographics—can establish the startup as an authority in its industry and spark audience engagement.

Crafting a Targeted Marketing Strategy.

Understanding the Target Audience.
In the 90-day startup launch, time is a luxury, and targeting the right audience is paramount. Entrepreneurs should conduct thorough research to understand their target demographic's behaviors, preferences, and pain points.

Building Anticipation.
Creating anticipation and excitement leading up to the launch is a strategic move. Teaser campaigns, countdowns, and sneak peeks can pique the audience's curiosity and keep them engaged in the lead-up to the big day.

Tapping into Influencer Marketing.
Collaborating with influencers or thought leaders in the industry can lend credibility and expand the startup's reach. For a 90-day startup, influencer partnerships can swiftly introduce the offering to a broader audience.

Utilizing Paid Advertising.
Paid advertising offers a way to quickly reach a targeted audience. Platforms like Google Ads and social media ads can help startups capture the attention of potential customers and drive traffic to their website.

Building Anticipation for Launch

Creating a Buzz.
Generating buzz requires a combination of creativity and strategic planning. Startups can use teaser videos, behind-the-scenes glimpses, and captivating visuals to build excitement among their audience.

Pre-launch Engagement.
Engaging the audience before the official launch fosters a sense of ownership and community. Contests, giveaways, and interactive campaigns encourage customers to participate actively and become invested in the startup's success.

Leveraging Early Adopters.

Early adopters are instrumental in driving initial interest and adoption. Entrepreneurs can offer exclusive access or benefits to early adopters, incentivizing them to become brand advocates and help spread the word.

The Grand Launch

Maximizing Impact.

The launch day is the culmination of the startup's efforts, and it should be executed with precision. Entrepreneurs should ensure that all marketing materials, social media posts, and communications align with the brand identity and message.

Leveraging PR and Media Coverage.

Securing media coverage—whether through press releases, media outreach, or partnerships—can amplify the startup's visibility and credibility. Media mentions add a layer of validation to the launch.

Monitoring and Responding to Feedback.

As the launch unfolds, entrepreneurs should actively monitor customer feedback and engagement. Rapidly responding to inquiries, comments, and concerns demonstrates a commitment to customer satisfaction.

Conclusion

The 90-day startup journey reaches its crescendo in the exhilarating moment of launch. Effective branding, strategic marketing, and a meticulously planned launch strategy are the catalysts that transform a startup's vision into a tangible reality. By creating a compelling brand identity, establishing a strong online presence, and crafting a targeted marketing campaign, entrepreneurs can ignite anticipation and excitement among their target audience. In the subsequent chapters, we delve into the intricacies of building and leading a cohesive team, nurturing an entrepreneurial mindset, and navigating the dynamic challenges of the 90-day startup landscape. These elements collectively contribute to the realization of a thriving business within the accelerated time frame.